TUMELO'S SAFARI CHRISTMAS ADVENTURE

By: K.A. Mulenga

© Kalenga Augustine Mulenga

TUMELO'S SAFARI CHRISTMAS ADVENTURE

Published by Kalenga Augustine Mulenga

Johannesburg, South Africa

augustine@kamulenga.com

ISBN 978-0-6398953-9-0

eISBN 978-0-6398954-0-6

2 4 6 8 10 9 7 5 3 1

Illustration and layout by Boutique Books

Printed in South Africa by Bidvest Data

I dedicate this book to my wife Sheba and my kids, Grace, Malaika and Kalenga Jr.

Thank you for believing in me!

In the heart of the African savannah, a young elephant named Tumelo stood under the warm sun, his trunk swaying in excitement. Christmas was just around the corner, and everyone in the animal kingdom was preparing for the big day. But this year, Tumelo wanted to do something special. He wanted to find the perfect gift for his family.

One morning, Tumelo met his best friends, Kendi the giraffe and Pula the zebra, by the river.

"I wish I could find something magical for Christmas," Tumelo said, a little unsure. "Something that will show my family how much I love them."

Pula's ears perked up. "I heard a story from the elder animals," he said. "There's a magical baobab tree deep in the savannah that grants Christmas wishes!"

"Do you think it's real?" Kendi asked, stretching her long neck to look around.

"It's worth a try," said Tumelo. "Let's find it!"

So off they went, across the vast savannah, with the tall golden grass tickling their legs and the bright blue sky stretching above them. Tumelo, Kendi and Pula walked for hours, laughing and chatting as they passed acacia trees and herds of antelope.

After a while, they came to a large and ancient baobab tree. Its trunk was wide and twisted, and its branches reached up to the sky like giant hands. Tumelo's eyes grew wide. "This must be it," he whispered.

Suddenly, a soft voice spoke from the tree. "Welcome, little ones," it said. "I am the Baobab of Wishes. Each of you may make a Christmas wish, but remember, the best gifts come from the heart."

Tumelo, Kendi and Pula looked at each other, excited but thoughtful. They each had something special they wanted, but the tree's words made them pause. What could they wish for that would truly show how much they cared?

Kendi was the first to step forward. "I wish for my family to have a Christmas feast, with all their favourite foods, so we can spend time together and share stories."

The baobab tree shimmered, and the air filled with the sweet smell of fresh leaves and fruit.

Pula then stepped up. "I wish to give my family the gift of music. A special song that will make them smile and dance."

Once again, the tree sparkled, and they could hear the faint sound of joyful music carried by the wind.

Finally, Tumelo thought hard. He loved his family and wanted them to know it. He stepped closer to the tree. "I wish for a star," Tumelo said, "to light up our home and remind my family of how much I love them, even when it's dark."

The tree glowed brightly, and a shining star appeared in Tumelo's trunk.

"Thank you," Tumelo said, beaming.

With their magical gifts, the friends hurried back home, eager to share their surprises.

That Christmas, the savannah was filled with the sound of laughter, music and love. Tumelo's star shone brightly, reminding everyone that the greatest gifts come from the heart and are best shared with the ones you love.

And so, the savannah animals celebrated, not just with presents, but with the gift of friendship, love and giving.

THE END

By K.A. Mulenga

Chuck the Cheetah

Cam, the Courageous Camaro

David, the great king

Donk and the Stubborn Donkeys

Drew, the Dragon

Elaine the Elephant

Four seasons in one day

Harry the Honest Horse

Imbwa, the Story Of the Dog and His Harsh Master

Jesus, the Baby King

Joe Finds His Way Home

Max the Gorilla

Malaika and the Magic Christmas Tree

Monty the Monkey and the Missing Rhinos

Never Give Up

Never Give Up 2 - The Miracle Game

Never Give Up 3 - Even Goalkeepers can Score

Never Give Up 4 - The Topsy Turvy Cup Match

Never Give Up 5 - The Comeback Match

Never Give Up 6 - It Was Meant To Be

Never Give Up 7 - The Amazing Adventure

Fatty the Pink Pug

Piggly the Angry Piglet

Polly the Polecat

Robbie the Raven and Debbie the Dove

Rudy, the Reindeer Who Could Not Fly

Spike and Spud , the Spaceboys

Susie Strickland, Sizzling Striker

Susie Strickland, Sizzling Striker 2 - The New School

The Christmas Cookie Contest

The Leopard Licks Its Spots

The Lion and the Impala

The Weaver Birds

Tumelo's Safari Christmas Adventure

Will and His Best Friend Whale

Thank you for reading Tumelo's Safari Christmas Adventure. I hope you enjoyed it! Please let K.A. Mulenga know about what you thought about the book by leaving a short review on Amazon, it will help other parents and children find the story. (If you're under 13, ask a grown up to help you)

Top Tip: Be sure not to give away any of the story's secrets!

Sign up to my readers' club weekly newsletter.
Simply click on the YES, SIGN ME UP button on my website.
I will never share your email address. Unsubscribe at any time.